GIFT OUT OF AFRICA

Bearing and Sharing the Gifts of God in You

Karen Kossie-Chernyshev, PhD

"Out of Egypt I Called My Son"
(Matthew 2:14)

Outskirts Press, Inc.
Denver, Colorado

Outskirts Press, Inc.
http://www.outskirtspress.com

ISBN: 978-1-4327-1155-9

Library of Congress Control Number: 2008943720

Outskirts Press and the "OP" logo are trademarks belonging to Outskirts Press, Inc.

PRINTED IN THE UNITED STATES OF AMERICA

Dedication

*To my dear husband, Oleg Chernyshev, MD, PhD,
and our precious gifts,
Daniel and Sofia*

Table of Contents

Karen Kossie-Chernyshev, PhD, is a professor of history at Texas Southern University, where her research focuses on African-American history and religion in the African Diaspora. She is also the minister of music at the Latter Day Deliverance Revival Center, Houston, TX, where her father, Bishop Roy Lee Kossie, is founder and pastor. She holds a dual BA in French and English (Rice University), an MA in French (Michigan State University); an MA in history (Rice University); and a PhD in history (Rice University). She speaks French, Spanish, and Russian, and she has studied, traveled, and conducted research in Western Europe, the Americas, Scandinavia, Eurasia, and off the coast of Africa.

Introduction

This inspirational book is designed to give readers a sustained opportunity to meditate on the gifts that God has placed inside them. The idea for the project came to me the night after Christmas 2002, a wonderful holiday that I was simply not ready to say good-bye to. To prolong the excitement, I decide to spend some time focusing on what happened to Jesus and His family after His celebrated birth, after the wise men had returned to their respective countries and the angels had stopped singing. The journey was an eye-opening one, as the young family was forced to go into hiding to protect God's gift to the world. When my eyes fell on the words "Out of Egypt I called My Son," I thought, "Wow! Jesus was called out of Africa!"

As I am a scholar of African-American history and the African Diaspora, the notion of Africa as a place of protection for the Christ child captivated me instantly and catalyzed the uplifting meditation that follows. I was so inspired that I requested permission from my pastor to share my thoughts in a three-part series during Black History Month. The series then became the foundation for the current book project.

I have organized the book into nineteen "meditations" because I want it to provide an inspirational bridge from Christmas to the Easter season, a wonderful four-and-a-half-month period of great expectations, renewed hopes, fresh starts, and enthusiastic commitments to self-improvement. I use the word "medi-tation" deliberately because I want readers to think carefully and prayerfully about their respective gifts as they journey with the Holy Family to and from Africa. They learn from the Holy Family's experience that using our gift areas for the glory and honor of God requires prayerful planning, action, and most of all obedience to the Word and will of God. My ultimate prayer is that readers will be inspired to stir up their respective gifts now and forever.

Overview

Bearing and Sharing the Gift

**Part I:
Bearing the
Gift**

**Divine Flight
Commands
(Itinerary provided)**

Matthew 2:13: Now they had departed, behold, an angel of the Lord appeared to Joseph in a **dream** saying, "Arise, take the young child and his mother, flee to Egypt and stay there until I bring you word, for Herod will seek the young child to destroy him."

**The Flight to Egypt
(Purpose of the trip)**

Matthew 2:14-15: When he arose, he took the young Child and His mother by night and departed for Egypt and was there until the death of Herod, that it might be fulfilled which was spoken by the Lord through the prophet saying, "Out of Egypt I called My Son."

Part II: Sharing the Gift

The Return Home (Mission accomplished)

Matthew 2:19-21: Now when Herod was dead, behold, an angel of the Lord appeared in a **dream** to Joseph in Egypt, saying "Arise, take the young child and His mother, and go to the land of Israel, for those who sought the young child's life are dead." Then he arose, took the child and his mother, and came into the land of Israel.

Part I:
Bearing the Gift

> **Matthew 2:13:** *Now they had departed, behold, an angel of the Lord appeared to Joseph in a* **dream** *saying, "Arise, take the young child and his mother, flee to Egypt and stay there until I bring you word, for Herod will seek the young child to destroy him."*
>
> **Matthew 2:14-15:** *When he arose, he took the young Child and His mother by night and departed for Egypt and was there until the death of Herod, that it might be fulfilled which was spoken by the Lord through the prophet saying, "Out of Egypt I called My Son."*

Meditation 1:
Announcing the Gift

Angelic Birth Announcements

Therefore the Lord himself will give you a sign: Behold, the virgin shall conceive and bear a Son and shall call his name Immanuel (Isaiah 7:14, Nelson Study Bible).

I love getting birth announcements in the mail. As soon as I open them, I start beaming and reading the announcement in an adult baby voice, especially when a fresh photograph is enclosed. During this moment of sheer exhilaration over the newborn, tummy aches, colds, and soiled diapers do not come to mind. Only the fresh scent of baby powder and lotion fills my imagination. Whether the little one is a girl or boy, I am simply elated that a new life has entered the world, perhaps to make it a better place.

I must admit, however, that I would be more than astonished if a complete stranger showed up at my doorstep to "inform" my husband and me that we were about to have a child. My amazement would no doubt continue if the messenger then began to offer specific instructions for raising this little person whom I had not seen or, for that matter, requested.

A number of biblical couples received divine pre-natal announcements from angels or prophets. Samson, Samuel, and Jesus were announced before conception. In the Old Testament, such persons were called "Nazarites" because God preordained them for a particular spiritual mission or purpose.

The advent of others was announced in dreams. Modern psychologists associate dreams with the subconscious, but many Christians believe dreams may also offer glimpses into the past, present, and future in ways that defy scientific explanation. These dreams are categorized as "divine" when they come or prove true. Many Christians believe God continues to send special agents into the earth to accomplish divine missions. In some cases, parents are given prophetic dreams and affirmations regarding their children before they are born. At other times, they get a post-natal affirmation that the child is indeed chosen of God.

Joseph and Mary's story is full of prophetic announcements delivered before and after Jesus' birth. All reaffirmed God's purpose for the Christ child. Joseph and Mary are excellent role models for contemporary Christian parents. Both were spiritual enough to hear the voice of God. Both were obedient enough to obey His command. Both had faith enough to take God at His word. Both made long-term personal sacrifices to bear Jesus Christ, the gift of God, the very Word of God made flesh.

While I am fully persuaded that there is only one Jesus—the Son of God—I am equally convinced that

God continues to plant "special agents" in the world to accomplish His will and purpose. Have you given birth to one of them? Are you willing to bear a living, breathing gift from God? What has God called you to be: an artist, musician, teacher, journalist, politician, medical doctor, businessman, mother, writer, or any combination of the aforementioned? Or has God called you to pioneer a novel profession yet to be named and appreciated? Do not be afraid to embrace godly dreams. God will give you the strength you need to realize every dream He plants inside you. In order to do so, however, you must "name" your gifts as they emerge—one by one!

Meditation 2:
Naming the Gift

O ne very fruitful couple had so much trouble deciding what to name their tenth child that they simply called him "boy" for the first three months of his life. Perhaps they simply had not planned for this one and were too busy with their other nine children to put much thought into naming their new addition.

Parents who plan their families generally spend considerable time trying to select their children's names before their little ones are born. Some buy name books and dictionaries to get meaningful ideas. Others honor family traditions, naming their children for revered relatives and friends. Still others select biblical names, hoping the children will share the traits of characters like Mary, Lydia, Priscilla, Joseph, Daniel, Luke, and even Jesus. Others create unique names to celebrate concepts or famous leaders.

When God intended to plant "special spiritual agents" in the earth, He was very clear about what they should be called. Their names preceded their earthly pilgrimages. They were named before they were born because their purpose was fixed—utterly unalterable. These gifts from God were literally programmed to execute a particular mission.

Jesus' birth announcement and name preceded even His conception. God's gift to the world was named "Emmanuel," "God with us." His name was an expression of His character and purpose. He was the "gift" and the "gifted" all at the same time. While none of us is the "the Word made flesh," Jesus prophesied that some would do greater works than even He on the earth. Contemporary ministers like Billy Graham, Benny Hinn, T.D. Jakes, Joel Osteen, and Joyce Meyer have certainly preached to larger crowds than Jesus, although none would have a "Christian" message without Christ's birth, death, and resurrection.

Sometimes the gift of God in us is very obvious, preceded by angelic announcements, visions, and dreams. At other times, parents and children alike are not aware of certain abilities or their use because "the fullness of time" has not come. Sometimes the gift is so intrinsic to the person that she cannot see her own giftedness, even while it stands out clearly to others. Others realize something beyond parental influence or environment defines the person in question. Something in them is born of God.

It may take awhile to identify gifts because they may not be traditional, public, or immediately visible. But such gifts can still be very powerful. Like the mortar that holds the bricks in place, some people are "Samsonites." They have unheard-of strength to carry on despite circumstances that would dampen the faith of most. Others are like rivers of living water. Every time you go around them, you feel refreshed and uplifted. Some are portable treasures of wisdom and knowledge. You always learn something around them whenever you meet them. When you talk to them, you feel as if you have just earned a PhD in thirty minutes of conversation. They are gifted with knowledge.

Some are loaded with spiritual gifts. Both Mary and Joseph had the gift of "faith." Faith was so strong in their lives that they were able to "receive" together the "gift of God" for the entire world. God entrusted them to raise the best gift the world has ever received—the promise of eternal life through Jesus Christ, the Savior of the world. There was nothing externally special about either of them. Joseph was a carpenter, and Mary, a virgin. But their individual and combined faith was extraordinary. As with them, the Lord could be using your gift of faith in Him to bring salvation to your entire household and to help others believe God for the impossible.

Educators throughout the country appreciate Harvard University Professor Howard Gardner's rubric for identifying gift areas in children.[1] His theory of multiple intelligences allows teachers and parents alike to value the myriad gifts students bring to the classroom—harbingers for the direction their lives should go. Consider Gardner's outline. In what areas do your children show exceptional ability? What is your gift? Is it your winning personality or good looks? Is it music or administration? Are you loaded with gifts to use for God's glory? What gift has He entrusted to you without your even asking for it? What part of God's divine mission has He assigned you or your loved ones to fulfill?

Meditation 3:
Confirming the Gift

Old Testament prophets like Isaiah foretold Jesus' birth and ministry. New Testament prophets like Anna and Simeon confirmed His arrival. Anna and Simeon offered what some Christians might call "right now" words from God to reassure Joseph and Mary about their very special son. When God has a special purpose in you, very often He will send Annas and Simeons into your life to confirm His purpose in you or your children.

When I was a young adult already playing the organ and directing the choir at my father's church, my mother informed me that a church mother had prophesied that I would play for the church. She said she withheld telling me because she knew that if the prophecy was indeed from God, He would surely perform His word. In addition, she did not want me to be unduly influenced by the pronouncement as I was still a child. She noted that at the time the prophecy was given, I was not tall enough for my feet to "touch the linoleum floor underneath the piano bench." I do not recall that prophetic moment. However, in retrospect, I do recall the day the Lord revealed my musical gift to me, although I was still too young to realize what was going on at the time.

I was in third grade. Having finished my work early, I asked one of my favorite teachers, Mrs. Atkinson, if I could look through the course songbook, and she agreed. "John Henry" looked interesting, but "On Top of Spaghetti" stole my attention. Inspired by the colorful picture of a huge plate of spaghetti covered with juicy meatballs, I looked at the song and began to sing. My teacher looked over my shoulder and asked me how I knew the song. I said innocently, "I just looked at these little dots on the lines and started singing." With no formal knowledge of music, I did not realize the "little dots" were "notes" on a music staff. Somehow, I understood the melodic and rhythmic relationship between the notes without a textbook explanation. I remember wondering why my teacher looked astonished at what seemed to me to be a logical decision: Follow the dots on the lines!

I also recall being drawn to the piano. In my spare time, I started picking out choir songs in three-part harmony. My first number and an all-time family favorite was Aretha Franklin's famous "How I Got Over" (*Amazing Grace*, 1972), a spirited version of Clara Ward's 1951 release. Of course, now, I do not have to "look back and wonder," as the lyrics declared. I know that the Lord placed musical gifts and others inside me. Some were being revealed; others were to be revealed.

Within a year, I had taught myself to play the piano by placing a chart behind the keys and asking my oldest sister Viki to show me the direction of sharps and flats. Convinced that I was serious about playing, my mother sent me to take piano lessons with a neighborhood piano teacher, now Dr. Bonnie Green, pastor and founder of Bible Refuge Temple, Houston, TX. By the time I ended lessons with her, I had started playing for one of the church's singing groups. The group encouraged my songwriting skills by singing some of my original compositions.

In subsequent years, the Lord sent one messenger after the other to reconfirm his purpose in my musical abilities. When I entered Rice University, to keep me encouraged, He had my music instructors, including the late Professor and Composer Paul Cooper, comment positively on my composition skills and musicality. My mother also bought me songbooks by Bill and Gloria Gaither and Andrae Crouch, whose melodic structures I am sure influenced my style and approach. Over the years, the Lord has continued to unveil abilities to sing, compose more complex compositions, and play new instruments.

Interestingly enough, my parents did not make me take lessons; I gravitated to them. They paid for five of nine children to take music lessons, but God's word stood firm. Karen, number eight, was destined to play. That is the way God preordained matters, and that is the way they shall remain. God is awesome! How I praise Him for granting me musical gifts to glorify His name! What gifts has He given you?

Meditation 4:

Protecting the Gift

No matter how beautiful the rose bush, it will die if it is not carefully protected from conditions that threaten its survival. To what length are you willing to go to protect your gift?

Consider Joseph and Mary's dilemma. The angels had sung, and the wise men from the east had borne their gifts of gold, frankincense, and myrrh, and returned home. Joseph and Mary were beaming over their divine child, "so holy, meek, and mild." They were preparing to raise the Son of God, their beautiful bundle of blessings. Perhaps Joseph went to sleep smiling, no doubt proud of his Son and proud of his wife, who now looked more breathtaking to him than ever.

Just as he was about to snuggle into dreams of fatherhood under warm covers of comfort and security, just as he was about to appreciate the financial blessings that had come his way to support his little "gift," an angel of the Lord appeared to him in a dream that bore all the characteristics of a nightmare. The angel said, "Arise, take the young Child and His mother, and flee to Egypt, and stay there until I bring you word; for Herod will seek the young Child to destroy Him."

"Oh, my God," Joseph must have thought, "someone wants to kill my innocent child, the Savior of the world." Some situations are so heartless that you know the enemy is on the loose, trying to thwart a major plan of God. No human with a conscience, with a heart of flesh, could imagine such a thing. The biblical record proves this level of inhumanity to be part and parcel of man without Christ.

If your gift is truly from God, do not be surprised when the enemy tries to kill it. Do not be surprised when he attacks the young. This is why youth ministry is so important. It is often viewed as a training ground for bigger and better opportunities, but youth ministry should be a priority in every church because the children honed in youth ministries can be lights to their peers and begin to make meaningful contributions to society even before they become adults. Children need radical protection and love to ensure their future success. If the enemy cannot kill their gifts violently, he will try to kill them softly. He will use others to belittle, overlook, obscure, ignore, or even pervert them.

Regardless of the internal or external mechanisms he uses, the enemy's goal of utter destruction will not succeed. God has a city of refuge built just for you. It may not look great from the outside, but it will be a place of protection and peace.

How I appreciate my parents for keeping a watchful eye over my sisters, brothers, and me. I was always surprised at how well they knew each of us and made a concerted effort to "train us up in the way that we should go," or according the gifts they saw expressed in us, even at an early age. I recall vividly the moment my mother handed me a teal diary with gilded pages and sparked through that simple but important gift my enduring love for writing.

I also remember well how my father insisted that the older children permit my younger sister Kimberly to express her toddler ideas during animated family discussions. He intervened intermittently and insisted that we "Let that baby talk!" In so doing, he was paving the way for her to become the radio personality, anointed youth pastor, and gifted evangelist she is today. Like Joseph, my father took an important step to protect her gift—one that has indeed made room for her and brought her before great women and men from throughout the world.

Joseph's experience reminds us that when your dreams turn into nightmares, the trials you face are not just about you, although your sleep may have been disturbed or you may have been forced out of your comfort zone. Your trials are really about the "gift" that God has planted in you to nurture, cherish, and protect.

You may be sleeping comfortably, so it seems, but the Lord knows there is eminent danger around; a prowler is on the loose. Wake up! Everything seems to be going well, but it is not. Like Joseph, you may be around family and friends and near all of your favorite places, but you must be prepared for an unexpected wake-up call.

Notice how compliant and obedient Joseph was. Consider earlier elements of his story. The Lord told him not to worry and that his fiancée was bearing the

Son of God. He must have taken a lot of heat for that one. The Lord told him to marry a girl who was already pregnant. Some would have insisted that Joseph was weak, a wimp, or whipped.

The Bible affirms that Joseph was willing to do what was necessary to protect his Son. He was even willing to sacrifice the attention that newlywed men look forward to after marriage—that blissful, sometimes short-lived period when their wives remain childless and can therefore be attentive to their every need. Breakfast in bed, morning massages—all roads lead to them. But Joseph had to forego perfect circumstances in order to protect the Gift of God. Doing the right thing might have made him look "wimpy" to others, but he was not worried. He knew that he was protecting the precious Rose of Sharon.

What gifts have you been assigned to protect? What steps have you taken to ensure their safety?

Meditation 5:

'Twas the Night After Christmas': Caring for the Gift

The angel of the Lord said, "Arise, take the young Child and his mother, flee to Egypt, and stay there until I bring you word: for Herod will seek the young Child to destroy Him."

Very often when we read the Christmas story, we end it at Jesus' birth, enjoy all the gifts we receive for His birthday, and then head for the New Year. We often forget that immediately after Jesus' advent, His family faced a tremendous trial. Caring for Him required the full cooperation of both parents. Had the Lord asked Joseph to go to Egypt alone, there would have been no problem. He could have "roughed it" like a man. But he was told to "flee" with a "child" and the baby's "mother." The command almost seems contradictory. Even the escape itself was complicated. It was one matter to flee alone, but altogether another to flee with a postpartum woman and her newborn child. The woman had been weakened physically and emotionally by childbirth, the baby was likely to cry and bring attention to the great escape, and all were vulnerable to seen and unforeseen circumstances.

Unlike Moses' mother, who put her son in a basket and sent him down the river, where he was found by Pharaoh's daughter, Joseph was commanded to take his wife and the baby with him. The family traveled as a complete unit. He was not instructed to send Jesus alone or with his mother to live with Aunty for a while, but rather to flee with both to safety. The Lord wanted the family unit to be intact physically to handle this particular trial. Obedient to the command of God, Joseph provided a spiritual covering for the child and his mother.

Mary's love for Joseph must have grown stronger with each trial. Joseph was an unselfish man. He did not shirk from his responsibilities, though he had been asked to undertake an unplanned journey. He realized that the journey was not about him, but about protecting the Gift that God had entrusted to his care. The destiny of "Mary's baby," the Light of the world, was tantamount.

Joseph is what many women would call "a good man." First, he did what he could to protect Mary from embarrassment. Then, he did what he must to protect a child who technically was not even his.

Thank God that there are still men with Joseph's caring and generous spirit. God has given them the spiritual wherewithal to act as surrogate fathers for children whose fathers are physically, spiritually, or emotionally absent from their children's lives for a variety of reasons, not limited to death or neglect. These men, like Joseph, are gifted with "charity," the ability to care for and love others selflessly and abundantly—the greatest gift of all!

How committed are you to caring for your gift? What sacrifices must you make to ensure its survival and continued growth?

Meditation 6:

Concealing the Gift

Our faith and trust in God as well as our ability to "hear" and "obey" the voice of God are significant. Joseph responded to his dream immediately. "He left by night" to protect Jesus. At certain stages of our gift development, the Lord requires that we work out His plan by night, when others are unconscious or unaware of what we are doing. Sometimes letting others know what we are doing, when we are going to do it, and how is not wise depending on the circumstances.

Have you ever had the Spirit of God lead you not to share a particular plan or aspect of your plan with others? I certainly have. Believe it or not, there are some gift snatchers out there. Revealing your plans to the wrong people at the wrong time opens the door to discouragement, theft, or destruction.

We cannot tell everyone everything all the time. Yes, American culture is a very open one. People accept invitations to talk shows and tell everything to the world in the name of sharing and being open. Yes, there is a time to testify so that others and we might be strengthened by God's blessings on our lives. However, we must be careful not to reveal too much too soon.

Regarding acts of charity, the scripture admonishes us not to let the left hand know what the right hand is doing (Matthew 6:3). The scripture continues: "And Your Father who sees in secret will Himself reward you openly" (Matthew 6:4). Simply put, some aspects of our divine mission are to remain secret if we want God to bless our efforts. They are between you and the Lord alone. The Lord has His own special way of dealing with you and developing your gift.

If you have a problem keeping a secret, pray and ask God to help you hold your peace on certain matters. Court records are full of cases where plaintiffs sought punitive damages for ideas, lyrics, passages from manuscripts, patents, and a host of other effects they claim others stole from them. In many instances, the person seeking redress might have saved himself the agony of litigation had he simply kept quiet about his plans. Somehow, the person managed to share his idea with the wrong person or in the wrong setting.

A popular gospel choral arrangement by Walter Hawkins proclaims, "Don't wait till the battle is over. Shout now!" Yes, shout now. Praise God for his goodness, but talk later unless the Lord instructs you to do otherwise. Some divine missions are overt, but many others are covert. Sometimes the Lord requires that we *speak* to the rock. At other times, as with Joshua and the battle of Jericho, he requires *silence* until an appointed time.

I am not encouraging paranoia or distrust, but rather emphasizing the importance of praying for the patience to speak a word in season and act in God's time. Joseph obeyed the voice of God. He did not bring attention to himself or his mission. He left in the night.

Think of how vulnerable Joseph and his family were. It was dark, and no one knew where he was going or why. For safety reasons, one of the first things we do when we are going out of town is tell family members or a trusted neighbor. If we are traveling to distant countries for prolonged visits, we even alert our banks or credit card companies so that they expect transactions from a certain location or red-flag those out of character with our pattern of spending. For safety reasons, we share our itinerary with co-workers or our bosses so that they know when we are leaving, when we arrive at our destination, and when we should return. We take these precautions to protect ourselves. We want someone to come looking for us if we do not arrive or return at a preset time or place. We may not tell everyone, but we usually inform a significant someone of our whereabouts. Families have averted or been alerted to grave dangers in this manner.

Joseph could not tell anyone about his journey because it was a divine <u>secret</u> mission, not a vacation. He was spiritually enlightened, but he had to keep others in the dark about his plans. Joseph was fleeing to protect the Christ-child—soon to be our Savior.

God bless Joseph! Imagine the great faith it must have taken to awaken his family in the middle of the night to journey southward to Egypt—with no midnight train to Egypt available. Joseph, with his family in tow, set out on a long arduous walk to a country where his ancestors had once been enslaved. How profound. Africa had been their place of enslavement, but now it represented hope. The absence of light made the journey perilous. Joseph and his family could have been robbed by midnight prowlers or attacked by beasts of prey, but he dared to embark upon this journey during a very vulnerable period in the lives of Jesus and Mary because God had instructed him to do so.

Perhaps Mary was still healing from childbirth, or Jesus' immune system was still weak. She and the Christ child could have experienced complications resulting from her exposure to the elements. What faith and courage it took for Joseph to initiate this journey in the middle of the night. He was able to do so because past experiences had convinced him that God was faithful to perform His word. The midnight escape would have meant certain doom for others, but it was Jesus' pathway to life.

Has the Lord required you to take a secret journey in the middle of the night? Pray that He will give you the courage to carry out the task assigned you. The idea may be unsettling, a little frightening, or even bordering on the insane in the minds of others. But be patient. Everything will be clear in God's time. The sun will soon shine on your pathway. Your gift will soon make room for you and bring you before great men!

Website:
The Holy Family in Egypt:
Http://www.middleeast.com/holyfamily.htm

Meditation 7:

Bearing the Gift

Of all the places the Lord could have sent the Holy Family, why did He send them to Egypt? Egypt had been a place of bondage for the children of Israel. Joseph's ancestors had been enslaved in Egypt for 400 years, and God had delivered them. In fact, some of his ancestors had even lost their lives looking back at Egypt and wishing for its fleshpots as the children of Israel journeyed through the wilderness. Here, however, the angel of the Lord instructed Joseph to go to Egypt, to "return" to a place that no doubt represented historical pain and suffering.

In the minds of those who knew of his flight, Joseph might have appeared to be regressive rather than progressive. Can you hear Joseph's detractors? "He claims the Lord told him to flee to Egypt. God is progressive. We are moving forward. We have already crossed that bridge."

The apparent contradiction reminds us that sometimes the Lord requires us to take actions that make no sense whatsoever to onlookers or even to us. That is why we have to choose our confidants carefully and use wisdom with what we tell them given the circumstances. Sometimes even our family members or closest friends cannot always handle or appreciate the route that the Lord is taking us to fulfill His purpose in our lives.

How many of us have taken a detour that seemed to put us out of the way? The enemy would love to have us ignore detour signs and plunge to destruction. That one-hour detour did not seem so bad after all when you learned upon arriving home that the freeway had suddenly collapsed under the power of raging flood waters, perhaps carrying some to the grave. The detour that seemed like an inconvenience turned out to be a path to safety and life. That is what Africa represented for Jesus—safety and life.

Saint Mark the Egyptian Evangelist noted that the Holy Family traveled to Egypt, but he did not provide the details about their journey. His silence notwithstanding, Coptic Christians, converted as a result of Mark's witness, take great pride in the Holy Family's journey to Egypt. In many Western Christian circles, Egypt is an ongoing metaphor for bondage. Coptic Christians, however, focus on Egypt's ultimate salvation, reciting such Old and New Testament prophecies as Isaiah 19:19 and 25, Psalms 91:5-6, and Revelation 3:20 to support their witness.

Coptic Christians are proud that God chose their country as a haven for the Christ child during the most precious years of Jesus' life. The Lord did not send the family to Italy or Greece (Europe) but rather to Egypt (Africa). According to their account, the Holy Family dwelt in thirty "blessed areas," each with its own history of the miraculous. They believe that Mary herself blessed Egypt again with daily appearances in her church in Zaitoon, Cairo, to express her love for the country that welcomed her. They believe she intercedes on their behalf.

Many Western scholars question the validity of Coptic accounts because no written record of the journey exists. The journal has not been found, and none of the apostles recorded any reminiscences that Jesus' parents might have told them about the family's sojourn. But many Coptic Christians nonetheless believe Joseph left a travel journal detailing the near four-year Egyptian excursion. The details of the Coptic Christian testimony continue to offer a rich opportunity to deepen our appreciation for this significant point in the life of Christ. Whether or not to believe the Coptic Christian witness matters little. Coptic Christians believe their Redeemer not only lives, but also that He dwelt safely among their own at the most precious time in His life. What we know for sure is that the approximate four-year period the Holy Family spent in Egypt was a time of nurturing for Christ and bonding for the family in general. Joseph found a protected place for his family. Now Joseph and Mary were free to nurture God's gift to the world![2]

Has God required that you bear your gift in an unlikely place? Not to worry. He required the same of the Holy Family. Perhaps Joseph and Mary's faith had been strengthened by the earlier journeys of the three wise men from the east, who brought precious gifts from afar to honor Jesus despite His humble birth. Their long-celebrated successful journeys as well as that of Holy Family affirm not only that where God guides He will definitely provide, but also that those who believe in Him will never be made ashamed (Romans 10:11). Others would faint given the exacting requirements of your assignment, but you will not. You will flourish because He has already equipped you to achieve the impossible. You cannot lose because He has promised to supply all of your needs according to His riches and glory by Christ Jesus. Bear your gift confidently in the strength and wisdom of God.

Meditation 8:

Nurturing the Gift

Whistle While You Wait!

So, the Lord has sent you to Egypt. You have tried to deal positively with difficult circumstances. You have taken a few courses in Egyptian language and culture, and visited all the famous places. Your gift, like Little Jesus, has learned to walk and talk like an Egyptian. Maybe the Christ child in you has even performed a few miracles by the grace of God. The positive strides notwithstanding, you are ready to return home.

The Lord knows, however, that given the circumstances Egypt is still the best place for you right now. He knows that Herod must die before you return. Notice that the Lord did not kill Herod; He waited until Herod died. God sometimes uses the natural course of life to fulfill His purpose. He could have sent a plague or changed the heart of the king, but that was not in His divine plan this time. He knew that Joseph and Mary had already demonstrated uncommon faith. Now God was helping them develop patience.

Besides, what appears to be the right place at the right time may turn out to be the absolute wrong place at the wrong time. Jerusalem can seem like the place to be. All the recording studios are there; all the connections; all the friends and financial support you need. But it can be the wrong place given the season in your life or your assignment. The person or entity that the enemy has planted to snuff out your gift could be in the very place you are trying your best to go. Nurture the gift where you are, and let patience have her perfect work.

The angel instructed Joseph to "stay there until I bring you word." Live, eat, drink, and get to know people. Pull out the family photo album or pass out business cards. Wherever the Lord has you "laying over" until the turbulence passes, enjoy your visit as much as you can. Learn the native language, enjoy the food, and embrace the cultural experience. Buy a T-shirt and souvenirs, visit the historic places, and treat the journey like a vacation. After all, God has promised to make your wilderness like Eden (Isaiah 51:3). Be all you can be "until He brings you word." Continue to nurture your gift in the light of His love!

You cannot leave when folks back home invite you to come or those in the "foreign land" tell you to go. You have to stay there until "the Lord brings you word." Again, God was testing Joseph's faith and patience. Joseph had to stay spiritually focused enough to "hear the word of the Lord" concerning his next move. He had to continue to nurture his relationship with the Lord during his journey. He had to be even more sensitive to the voice of God in this "foreign land" with "strange gods" and different customs. Joseph did not realize his obedience would lead to the birth of an entire Christian tradition that continues to celebrate the Holy Family's journey to the cradle of civilization. He had to "stay there" in order for this inadvertent but historically noteworthy blessing to occur.

What does it mean to "stay there"? You might really want to go, and you may be feeling nostalgic or out of place, but stay there. Your money might be running low, and you know you could live better if you could just go back home to Momma and Daddy or Aunty, but stay there. You know you could make much more money working for your favorite company back home, but stay there. How long? "Until the <u>Lord</u> brings you word."

"Until" is a very open word. Many of us, especially westerners, want an exact date, day, and time. When we travel, we generally know ahead of time when we are going to return home. Our schedules are prearranged. Knowing that we have a return flight helps us to endure even when our journeys are difficult. We can see the end in sight. Joseph and Mary could not.

They did not have a precise schedule. "Until" was as precise as it got. Perhaps you are asking the Lord, "How long?" and He is not giving you an exact time. He's just saying "until." I know it is frustrating, particularly if you live in a society where time is money and money is time. What if the Lord says "until" to your time question? Can you handle the answer "until"? Can you let patience have its perfect work? You must, because in patience you possess your soul (Luke 12:19).

I will never forget a very vivid lesson the Lord

taught me about patience. One day I was speeding home from Bellaire Senior High School, Houston Independent School District (HISD), where I taught French at the time. As I approached Homestead Road, the major thoroughfare bordering my neighborhood, a very slow-moving driver crept in front of me to turn left onto the thoroughfare. I wanted badly to pass him, but the double yellow lines and the raised yellow lane divider prohibited me from doing so. I was complaining out of frustration because I wanted to make the light. It had changed from yellow to red, and I knew I could have made it across if only the car had gotten out of my way.

No sooner had I positioned my hand to honk my horn at the driver in front of me, when out of nowhere a speeding car zoomed through the intersection at about 85 mph in a 30-mph zone. My heart skipped a beat as I realized how close I had come to death. The slow-moving driver had, in fact, saved my life and perhaps that of the other driver as well. I thought the "tortoise" was impeding my progress, but God was using him to keep two impatient jackrabbits from becoming roadkill.

Do you have some projects that you are praying for the Lord to bring to closure, or some dreams you are waiting to fulfill? I understand. I have been there many times. I have worked on a number of projects for what I would certainly call "enough time," but the Lord is still saying "until." Perhaps your progress is not delayed due to your own inactivity. You have done everything in your power to pronounce a benediction on a particular undertaking. Or you may be doing a particular job totally out of the strength of God because it is not where you want to be. If so, continue to trust the Lord to sustain you miraculously "until." Wait until the Lord speaks directly to your heart before you move. Stay there until <u>He</u> sends you word even if others may not fully appreciate the gifts God has placed inside you. He promised never to leave us or forsake us (Hebrew 13:5). He also promised to be our very present help in the time of trouble (Psalm 46:1). God knows you are waiting on Him. Your patience and peaceful disposition are pleasing to Him. They are evidence of the perfect love and abiding trust you have in Him.

Just keep whistling praises while you wait. As with Joseph and his family, when you leave, those around you will realize someone special was among them. Do not be surprised if you become a model for others, or when a method, program, wing, or building is named in honor of your contribution. Just continue to nurture your gift where you are. Surely, the Lord's many blessings will overtake you shortly and encourage others to embrace the Blessed Hope![3]

Part II:
Sharing the Gift

Matthew 2:19-21: Now when Herod was dead, behold, an angel of the Lord appeared in a **dream** to Joseph in Egypt, saying, "Arise, take the young Child and His mother, and go to the land of Israel, for those who sought the young Child's life are dead. Then he arose, took the Child and his mother, and came into the land of Israel.

Meditation 9:
Unwrapping the Gift

Now when Herod was dead, behold, an angel of the Lord appeared in a dream to Joseph in Egypt, saying, "Arise, take the young Child and His mother, and go to the land of Israel, for those who sought the young Child's life are dead." Then he arose, took the young Child and His mother, and came into the land of Israel (Matthew 2:19-21, Nelson Study Bible).

How delighted Joseph and Mary must have been when they received a divine message that the coast was clear. They could now return home. Having lived in Egypt for a thousand days or more, they had probably developed some lasting friendships and connected with the culture. Now it was time to return to Israel. I can imagine how excited their friends and family members were to see them upon their return. They were perhaps most delighted to see how much Jesus had grown.[4] Certainly, they "ooh-ed" and "aah-ed" about this gifted little one and celebrated His arrival. Their kind words were no doubt encouraging to parents and child alike.

Isn't it great to have people around when you are unwrapping presents? The oohs and aahs in the background add to the experience and heighten the overall pleasure of being appreciated. I thank God that He sends people to help us unwrap and celebrate our gifts—those who are willing to "ooh" and "aah" over our gift areas. I definitely appreciate the encouraging words I receive from church members, especially Judy Jackson, Joyce Pope, Alice Hall, and her daughter, Rhonda, whom the Lord has used time after time to build my confidence in all areas of musical expression, personal presentation, or God's purpose for my life.

On the Sundays I feel least confident about my contribution to the service, Sister Judy tells me how blessed she is by my singing and playing, particularly my shouting music. She also makes special requests for selected original compositions, which any composer would appreciate. When I feel least attractive or thoroughly ambushed by the multifaceted demands of my life, Sister Joyce, as if on divine appointment, will come and give me a big hug and say, "Kay, you are so special," or my all-time favorite, "You really don't realize how beautiful you are." Or when I am feeling unsure about one or another undertaking, Sister Hall will inadvertently say, "Dr. Kay, I have been praying for you. Be encouraged. The Lord has great things in store for you." Rhonda, her daughter, has also shared encouraging prophetic words or dreams with me, one of which confirmed God's purpose in this current project. Timely affirmations like the ones these godly women continue to share are like apples of gold in pitchers of silver (Proverbs 25:11).

Celebrators like the aforementioned women are very special people because they help you go from glory to glory. They know that the paper, tape, trimmings, and bows must come off in order for the "gift" of God to be fully appreciated and used to magnify Him. They help you to keep believing that the best is yet to come. They help you to stay focused and grounded in the promises of God when others may expect very little to emerge from your plainly wrapped or very tiny box. They remind you that God has entrusted you with His most precious gift—salvation, one that will always bring out God's best in you.

Whether your gift is covered in comic strips or foil that understate your value, whether it is sealed with invisible or duct tape, praise God for your gift and welcome these special individuals who celebrate your unveiling.

Do you have people in your life who are willing to esteem and celebrate the gift of God as it unfolds in your life? If so, thank God for them and let them know how important their words of encouragement are to you. Celebrators are very important because they help us reveal to the world what is underneath all the wrapping paper and trimmings. Let's praise God for the "ooh-ers" and "aah-ers" in our lives. With their help we discover the gifted gems the Lord has called us to be. They really are the wind beneath our wings. May the celebrations never end!

Meditation 10:
Redirecting the Gift

But when he heard that Archelaus was reigning over Judea instead of his father Herod, he was afraid to go there. And being warned by God in a dream, he turned aside into the region of Galilee. And he came and dwelt in a city called Nazareth, that it might be fulfilled which was spoken by the prophets, "He shall be called a Nazarene."

Here we go again!" you say when a trial reinvents itself—a trial you thought was over. This was exactly Joseph's experience. Herod was dead, but his son was alive. The son obviously exceeded his father in his totalitarian quest for power because this time God himself warned Joseph in a dream. News of Archelaus's rise to power forced Joseph to redirect his plans. The circumstances Joseph and his family faced nonetheless served a spiritual purpose. His decision to dwell in Nazareth paved the way for the fulfillment of prophecy that *"[Jesus] shall be called a Nazarene."*

Detours are generally less direct paths to our various destinations. They can also be more adventurous than the frequently traveled road even though they take longer and are more complicated. They provide an opportunity to enjoy sights, scenes, and experiences that would have been missed on the well-beaten path.

As the Christ child's parents journeyed from place to place, he was being exposed to a variety of people, places, and things. He and his family were learning how to adapt to various circumstances, customs, and personalities—social skills that Jesus would definitely need in ministry. Given the unexpected nature of the Holy Family's flights to Egypt and now Galilee, all members were also learning about the grace and mercy of God, as they relied on the kindness of strangers to adjust to their new environments.

The Lord often directs us to take routes that really seem out of the way. They appear superfluous to us because we simply do not have His grand design in mind. We sometimes become anxious when the alternate path seems infinitely long even when He lets us know ahead of time and we initially accept His decision. Sometimes we begin to doubt ourselves if not God and say, "Surely, I must have made a wrong turn somewhere!" or "Perhaps I misunderstood what He told me." But when we pray to make certain that we are on track, the Spirit of God continues to reassure us that we are centered in His perfect will, though visible circumstances suggest we are in the middle of nowhere. God, in such circumstances, is simply building our faith and trust in Him, both of which are indispensable to our Christian walk.

I remember vividly when the Lord alerted me to one of my life's major detours. Although I had ac-

cepted His plan initially, I began to question God
about His plan as one year after the other passed.

Just before I headed to a Midwestern university to
earn a PhD in French, with a graduate fellowship in
hand, I dreamed I was driving along the freeway and
saw two exit signs. One was marked "France" and the
other "Jerusalem." I said, "I think I am going to go to
Jerusalem since I've already been to France." I had
lived and breathed everything French from my high
school days in Ms. Sherry Gidden Tobias's class,
which culminated with a two-week trip to Paris,
France, just before I headed to Rice University for
college. My parents appreciated Ms. Gidden Tobias's
positive influence because she was not only a dedicated French teacher but also a devoted Presbyterian
who encouraged me in my Christian walk and mod-
eled for me and other young people of various religious persuasions and backgrounds how to have good
clean fun.

With my parents' permission and the help of administrators, teachers, and classmates, I turned my
ten-dollar allowance into $2,000 dollars and initiated
the first of many journeys to the Hexagone. I had become so engaged in French by the end of my freshman
year that friends nicknamed me "Ms. International." I
loved French because of its musicality, French food
because it was delicious, French culture because of
France's creation of "la haute culture," "les parfums,"
"les beaux arts," and French people for their historic
embrace of African-American culture, particularly
during the Jim Crow era, a period of legalized racial
discrimination in the United States, dating roughly

from *Plessy v. Ferguson* (1896) to *Brown v. Board of Education* (1954).

When I spoke to my mother about the dream, she said, "Karen, I think the Lord is showing you that even though you really love French, you are ultimately going to choose His perfect will for your life." I kept the prophetic dream and her words in mind as I headed to graduate school. My career goal at the time was to work with the United Nations and ultimately to become an ambassador to a francophone country. But the more I studied, the more my desire to embrace things French began to wane. Feeling as if I were literally running out of gas, I decided to earn my Master's degree a semester early and then head home to rethink the course of my life.

Still trying to put the French to good use, thanks to Lynn Weekes Karegeannes, a dear college friend from South Carolina, I worked as a research assistant to Arianna Huffington as the acclaimed author, now political analyst, was putting the finishing touches on *Picasso, Creator and Destroyer* (1988). I taught French and English in the Houston Independent School District (HISD) at the Contemporary Learning Center (CLC), nicknamed "criminals last chance." Despite its less-than flattering dub, I met warm, dedicated professionals like Principal Norita Daniels and students who went on to live very productive lives. One young man whom I taught became a dynamic preacher. I also worked part-time for Rice University's School of Continuing Studies, officially renamed the Suzanne M. Glassock School of Continuing Studies in 2006.

In my spare time, I began making plans to work for the Peace Corps in francophone Africa. When I shared my plans with my mother, she frankly added, "Karen, you have a Peace Corps [opportunity] in your backyard." She was absolutely right. With her encouragement, I decided to pretend I was in West Africa and applied for a job in the North Forest Independent School District (NFISD), at one time the largest predominantly black district in Texas. As NFISD was the district of my intellectual and social birth, I taught there with a passion and in the company of many educators and administrators who had shaped my early development. I loved the experience and grew professionally and my students intellectually. The synchronicity was wonderful and inspiring.

I was pleased with God's choice, but some of my former classmates were not. One who had expected me to achieve grander goals was disappointed when he learned that I had returned to NFISD to teach. He was expecting a lot from me, as I was voted most likely to succeed and named valedictorian of Forest Brook High School's class of 1981, proudly labeled "The Class with Class." "I thought you would be in the White House by now," this disenchanted friend confided. I simply smiled and said, "Sorry to disappoint you," and continued my morning jog.

I was not just teaching, even though I certainly did not need to make an excuse for engaging in a very important profession. I was on a fascinating journey that was chock full of opportunities to grow. What seemed like a lack of progress was a God-ordained detour that was tremendously enriching. I knew I was at the center of God's will and continued to work peacefully there.

This former classmate did not know I had actually left the cherished teaching job to which he referred to pursue a PhD in history to write a book on a subject very dear to me—the history of African-American Pentecostalism-Charismaticism in the US Southwest. I did not pause to offer an explanation because I did not think I needed to defend my God-ordained choices.

My decision to write a book emerged during a nostalgic moment in the Midwest, where I was attending graduate school. Despite the nice people I met there, I missed the church mothers who had kept me smiling throughout my childhood with their kind words, dollar bills, and peppermint candy. Each of the following seasoned women helped me to appreciate the "straight and narrow way": the late Mothers Mamie Woods, my godmother; Jerline Satcherwhite, who worked with the youth and often encouraged the congregation with her rendition of "Count Your Blessings, Name Them One By One"; and Josephine Sanders, the mother of the church, who, among other things, made sturdy pound cakes and awesome pots of greens.

In addition to my father, the founder and pastor of the church, I also missed the elders and deacons who had kept me encouraged with their prayers, particularly the late Brother Clarence Johnson, who loved to have fun, worked faithfully with various renovation projects, and drove the church van. Full of longing for their familiar faces, I yearned to capture in words memories of people very dear to me.

My experience with Arianna Huffington gave me the confidence to begin writing. The opportunity was significant even though my primary job was to check footnotes—one of the last and least-coveted aspects of any book project. It provided me with the first official occasion to see my name in a publication other than a neighborhood newspaper, church program, school yearbook, or graduation announcement. How proud I was to be listed with a host of contributors from throughout the globe.

When I told Huffington's mother that I wanted to write a book, she recounted Arianna's path to her writing career and encouraged me to simply write. Of course, I could not help but chuckle at her suggestion that someone might give me an advance to write, as had been the case with Huffington's book on Maria Callas. I was not Arianna Huffington and African-American Pentecostals, with our vibrant music and affinity for polyrhythm, were a far cultural cry from Maria Callas. But I did follow through on her suggestion that I simply write.

I sent a copy of a 50-page manuscript to my mentor and friend, Dr. Linda McNeil, Rice University, who then put me in touch with Dr. John Boles, an award-winning scholar of Southern history and editor of the *Journal of Southern History*. Boles then encouraged me to conduct research on my subject at Rice University. He knew at the time that Vinson Synan's *The Holiness Movement in the United States* (1971) was the only book-length scholarly study that commented on the history of Black Pentecostals. Boles was sure that the study I proposed would add significantly to the academic literature, especially given my insider's position.

Despite Dr. Boles's invitation, I was so enjoying my teaching experience and so accustomed to teaching language and literature that it took me three years and a fresh nudge from the Holy Spirit to accept Boles's suggestion to apply, as well as to admit that I could not work on such an extensive book project while teaching secondary school full time. The Lord used a prophet to reconfirm His will.

A week before I received my acceptance letter from Rice University to attend graduate school, I stopped by a revival service conducted by Reverend Alfred Hinton of Muskogee, Oklahoma, and sponsored by Miracle Deliverance Holiness Church, Houston, TX, where Ezzie Mae Williams is founder and senior pastor. Hinton called me to the altar to pray for me and said, "I see you going back to school, and the Lord is going to bless you with the finances to do so. I see thousands of dollars coming into your hands." True to the prophecy, I was blessed with a fellowship to pursue my degree. God is awesome!

With the wind at my back, I entered Rice University for a second time in 1993 and enjoyed every minute of the journey. By 1997, I had witnessed Huffington's mother's assertion prove true. With dual status as a PhD candidate at Rice University and a visiting professor of history at Texas Southern University, where Nobel Laureate Toni Morrison once taught, I applied for and was awarded a dissertation fellowship from the National Endowment for the Humanities. The fellowship allowed me to dedicate a full academic year to researching and writing a near 400-page thesis on my beloved subject.

Certainly, I was grateful for God's many blessings, but I began to reevaluate the course of my life. I asked the Lord once again why He had allowed me to earn a BA and MA in French. Yes, I had used French to fulfill the requirements of my PhD and was informed that evaluators were impressed with my performance on the French language proficiency exam, but I knew that passing this examination could not have been God's only goal for my fluency. "What was that all about, Lord?" I continued to ask. "Why would you have me become fluent in a language and not use it at all? Why French, Lord? Why?"

The answer finally came when I met my Russian husband. When we decided to marry, I let him know how disappointed I was that I had not followed an earlier spiritual prodding to learn Russian, as I wanted to communicate with his relatives directly, especially with his mother. He said, "Oh, don't worry. My mother is a French teacher." I was speechless. French served and stills serves as our common language, although both of us have made considerable progress in the other's native tongue.

To doubly reaffirm that God had led me to learn French, neither my husband nor I knew that his Russian daughter would eventually reside in a francophone country. In short, I needed French to help unite our very international, cross-cultural, multilingual family. As a longtime mentor later affirmed, I was living my own version of the United Nations and acting as a "US ambassador" to my own international family. Fabulous!

Now that I have achieved a noteworthy end of my pursuit of French, I realize God had been leading me every step of the way. The journey to God's destination took more than ten years to complete, but the ride was wonderful and fulfilling. The experience convinced me that God uses our trials and triumphs to fulfill His purpose in us. Joseph was led to Nazareth so Jesus could be called a "Nazarene." I was led to study French so I could be called a "Chernyshev"!

Do not fret if God is redirecting your path. The detour is part of His divine plan for your life. Just sit back, enjoy the ride, and prepare for a sensational end.

Meditation 11:
Reconfirming the Gift

In those days, John the Baptist came preaching in the wilderness of Judea, and saying, "Repent, for the kingdom of heaven is at hand!" For this is he who was spoken of by the prophet Isaiah saying: "The voice of one crying in the wilderness: Prepare the way of the Lord; Make his paths straight" (Matthew 3:1-3, Nelson Study Bible).

Jesus' baptism was pivotal. He had to be confirmed before He began his public ministry. In accord with God's perfect will, His cousin John baptized Him. Through this public act, His calling was confirmed, and He accepted Himself as Lord and Savior. We must do the same if we want our gifts to serve the cause of Christ. We must embrace our own giftedness, not out of pride, but rather with confidence, great humility, and faith. We must take the added step, nonetheless, to confess our sins, ask forgiveness for them, and commit to daily growth in the grace of our Lord. We must also make a conscious effort to submit to God's divine plan for our lives daily.

Reconfirmation, especially public reconfirmation,

solidifies our giftedness not only for our own benefit, but also for the benefit of others. Our "coming out" publicly provides a solid foundation for future flourishing and helps others to respect and appreciate the new level of expertise or experience afforded to us. This is why we gladly invite others to wedding ceremonies, baby showers, graduations, ordinations, and other events highlighting the achievement of key milestones in our lives. The public nature of such reconfirmations is key because it provides the space for a collective witness to the God-given calling on our lives.

Reconfirmation provides the added assurance not only that a greater level of experience has been achieved, but also that the "gifted one" is qualified to pursue even higher goals. Reconfirmation provides important space for the newly established to be welcomed into the community of authorities in a given area. Veterans know from reconfirmation that the given individual is prepared to help nurture and sustain the tradition, mission, or undertaking in question. Reconfirmation assures those who are part of a given effort that capable leaders have been prepared to continue the vision or plan.

Such reconfirmation also provides important space for established members of a given community to re-evaluate the nature of their own historic role to a given mission. John understood and accepted that the time had come for him to decrease so that Jesus could increase.

Notice that Jesus did not confirm Himself. He waited on acknowledgement from His cousin John the Baptist, the leading minister of their region. At the same time, John the Baptist was totally submissive to the will of God. He realized that even while he had borne rich fruit in his season, his season was ending, and Jesus' season was just beginning. Thank God for John's example. He was willing to defer to the emerging call of God on someone else's life despite his own popularity. John knew that he had taken the people as far as he could. He preached repentance, an indispensable step to fellowship with God. But God had ordained Jesus to take humanity a step further. Only Jesus, the Word made flesh, could die for our sins and then send "The Comforter," the Holy Spirit, to guide us into all knowledge of the truth.

Rest assured that God knows exactly what will be the importance and impact of your gift to the world. Rest assured that He will send experienced, reputable witnesses like John the Baptist to reconfirm His will and purpose in your life so that others can experience and appreciate the gifts of God in you.

Meditation 12:
Operating the Gift

Like diamonds from Tiffany's and Godiva chocolate, some gifts are admired immediately, as soon as they are opened. Others cannot really be enjoyed until they have been properly assembled. What kind of gift has the Lord given you? Do you know how to operate it? After all, it is your "divine gift," not someone else's. The surest plan for working your gift comes from the "gift manufacturer," the Lord. What "divine" instructions came with your gift? Samson's parents were told never to cut his hair. The presence of God rested most heavily upon him through his hair. Has the Lord given you special instructions for operating your gift?

The Lord will send spiritual leaders and others to help you interpret the instructions. He sends local pastors and evangelists; radio, television, and cyber ministries; and everyday people to offer constructive words of encouragement and inspiration.

Once your gift is revealed, confirmed, and even re-confirmed, the Lord will also send people who have similar gifts and can therefore offer words of wisdom or advice as you operate the gift of God in your life. If you know God has gifted you to write, you can nurture that gift by taking writing courses on your preferred genre: fiction or non-fiction; travel and leisure; or sports writing. Even if the instructor is not a member of your particular religious denomination or persuasion, he or she is still "gifted" in that area and can offer advice that encouragers cannot.

Do not be surprised when you appear to outgrow your teachers. This is part of natural progression. Just remain respectful and grateful, knowing that what you have accomplished rests on the foundation laid by those who preceded you. After all, no man is an island, and no man stands alone. When it is time, the Lord will send you someone who can take you further along your journey. Jesus was able to converse with the rabbis at a very young age; however, He was still a child and needed to be trained. Mary and Joseph did not leave Him in the synagogue. They knew He still had some growing up to do despite His precocious nature.

Their actions suggest that parents should not minimize their role in shaping the lives of their gifted children. Their children might be gifted in one area but may need serious training and guidance in others. Parents provide balance for their children when they challenge them to strengthen the weak places as they continue to gain strength in their gift areas.

We should never be intimidated by our children's giftedness or let others make us feel as if our children need a different set of parents to realize their God-given potential. A lot of great people were born of parents who looked no more exciting than the couple on the cornflake box. You are exactly the couple or single parent God wants to use to nurture the gifts that emerged from a moment's loving embrace. You have been assigned to nurture your gifted children.

God will equip you with the stamina, patience, and the necessary life space to harness and nurture your children's gifts. Some parents lead lives that are so overwhelming that they inadvertently thwart their children's development. Parents who embrace their role as parents understand the importance of giving their children room to grow and come into their own. They are more than happy to let their children develop and shine, and never compete with them for the spotlight.

I am not suggesting that parents cannot benefit from the help of trained professionals, teachers, or others as they help their children hone their gifts and talents, but rather that parents should be confident in their ability to guide their children toward their God-ordained paths. Certainly, Joseph could not tell Jesus what it was like to be the Son of God based on experience. Yet he presented Jesus with an excellent model of faith and obedience, both of which helped Jesus fulfill His mission. Joseph embraced his role as the earthly father of "Jesus," God in the flesh. He protected Him until the Ultimate Gift was unveiled to the world. Let us pray for the strength and wisdom we need to emulate Joseph's example.

Meditation 13:
Growing in the Gift

As His custom was, He went into the synagogue on the Sabbath day, and stood up and read (Luke 4:16).

G rowing in our respective gift areas requires accepting where God wants us to grow, under whose leadership, and for how long. Yes, growing in our gift areas requires uniting in fellowship with a body of believers. Growing in our gift areas requires going to church as Jesus did. He went and participated actively in services on a regular basis.

Our modern, hi-tech world offers a variety of ways to grow spiritually. There are hundreds of radio and television programs, newsletters and magazines, cyberspaces and blogs, and all are great, innovative tools for growth and enrichment. Such modes are particularly helpful when Christians are suffering from physical challenges that prohibit them from attending church. They also help us to stay readily connected to people from throughout the world. But sustained Christian living requires being planted firmly in a church, in good soil, where a man or woman of God is committed to watching over our precious souls with tender love and care.

Some Christians argue that they can be fed spiritually from their living rooms or automobiles as well as from church. Even if that may appear to be true, we must surrender our contemporary interpretations to the Word of God, which admonishes us not to forsake the assembling of ourselves together as some choose to do (Hebrews 10: 25). It is at church that we are best able to encourage each other. The church is the house of God, our Father. It is where the family of God, the body of Christ, comes together to worship and praise God, and most importantly to hear His Word.

We belong to a "body" of believers that needs all of its parts. Our praises help complete the grand praise song that our particular congregation offers to God. Our strength and the tenor of our voices are missed when we are not in the number. Someone needs to hear our testimonies of faith. In fact, we will be strengthened by the words of our own testimonies of God's goodness. In addition, we need to hear the testimonies of others up close and personal. The church, a place of divine fellowship, is an excellent location for offering such pronouncements of faith and their reinforcement, anointed praise and worship.

Have you become bored with the routine of church? Are you finding yourself wanting to withdraw from church fellowship? If so, talk to the Lord about your hesitation and pray that He will bless you to reach a place in your spiritual life where you can proclaim as David did: "I was glad when they said unto me, come let us go into the house of the Lord" (Psalm 122:1). In so doing, you will ensure that your spiritual growth is steady and sure.

In the house of God, where the presence of God waters your soul and His light shines brightly on your pathway, your gifts can be nurtured on a regular basis and flourish bountifully in due season. Let's bask in the presence of the Lord of Lords. Let's give the glory to Christ our King—together and on one accord.

Meditation 14:
Testing the Gift

Man shall not live by bread alone, but by every word that proceeds from the mouth of God (Matthew 4:4).

One of my enduring childhood memories is of the emergency public service announcement that sometimes interrupted my favorite program, "Mr. Roger's Neighborhood," with an ear-piercing beep followed by a robotic pronouncement: "This is a test of the emergency broadcast system. This is only a test." Like fire drills in grade school, I found it hard to appreciate the wisdom gained from simulation and trial runs. Later, when I became an adult and teacher, I learned the intrinsic value of tests, which not only reveal our strengths and weaknesses, but also affirm whether or not we have mastered the material.

Just as Jesus was tried, we will undergo tests of our faith despite our will not to do so. Of course, we do not like tests namely because they acquaint us, sometimes painfully, with the depth of our shortcomings even in areas we thought we had mastered. Despite the difficulty associated with testing, the scripture assures us that the trying of our faith is more precious than silver or gold.

Many Christians are experiencing dramatic tests of their faith because of current social, political, environmental, and economic developments. On the Gulf Coast, before victims of Hurricane Katrina had found dry ground, many found themselves faced with Hurricanes Rita, Gustav, and most recently Ike. On the West Coast, residents in various enclaves have seen beloved neighborhoods engulfed in flames.

In the wake of Barack Obama's historic election as the first African-American President of the United States, many Americans still face discrimination in various forms. His campaign and election have energized millions with the themes of hope and change, but it will take determined action to erase the blight of poverty that plagues many urban and rural communities.

Because of dramatic economic downturn, hardworking families have watched their savings accounts and 401K's dwindle along with the hope of their children attending the universities of their choice. And the rate of unemployment has been steadily rising in the wake of economic duress. Some charitable organizations and megachurches have been forced to lay off employees, as they rely on donations from constituents who are themselves hunkering down for what may be a very long and cold economic winter. The American Dream has become a veritable nightmare for many.

In light of current difficulties and even tragedies, some are willing to admit that they have been ultimately strengthened by their trials, which have either acquainted them with or helped them develop resilience that they did not realize they needed or had. Others, particularly those who lost belongings through natural disasters, admit that they are learning in distress just how kind and loving even perfect strangers can be in their darkest hour.

This is true for my family. Our home was burglarized during Hurricane Ike as we and the families of other medical personnel on call took shelter in the Houston Medical Center. My husband and I had both sensed impending danger and did what we could to secure our home before we left, but thieves had the perfect cover. The house adjacent to ours had been vacant since we moved in, and Mr. Billy, our neighbor across the street who insisted on looking out for us, had died three weeks earlier. His house now stood quiet and empty, increasing our vulnerability. Our home security system was breached because the phone lines were down. A kind neighbor called the police as soon as she and her daughter saw the crime unfolding but access to the house was compromised by debris and trees felled by the storm. The police arrived a full hour after her call.

As my husband and I surveyed our home for damage, we heard our toddler start to cry when he realized the VCR on which he had watched American and Russian cartoon favorites was no longer there. He rolled on the floor in despair trying to understand what had happened. His Aunts Simmie and Kimberly came immediately to the rescue with video equipment so he could watch Veggie Tales, Cheburashka,

Sesame Street, and its Russian version—Ulitza Sesame.

As my husband and I pulled the house together, we were heartbroken when we realized almost four years of videotapes containing precious memories dating back to our son's birth had also been stolen. Certainly, we knew the material things could be replaced, but we also knew that emotional security was priceless.

We felt violated and were utterly outdone when we learned that at least two of the three thieves lived down street and may have been abetted by others who alerted them of our departure. Yes, we knew we lived in a community in transition. The Fifth Ward and Greater Fifth Ward regions had earlier produced Barbara Jordan, Mickey Leland, Ruth Simmons and hundreds of other highly productive African-American educators and professionals. But now residents, many of them aging, found themselves in an arduous struggle against economic downturn, the flight of young middle-class blacks to the suburbs, and the invasion of crack cocaine.

We were nonetheless astounded by the intruders' boldness and determination. Within a stone's throw of Mickey Leland Memorial Park and the home of an elected state official, they risked their lives in broad daylight, breaking through three barriers to take what did not belong to them. But church and family members who learned of our dilemma came to the rescue. Their ready help, prayers, and encouraging words eased our pain and rekindled our hope, as well as strengthened our determination to overcome evil with good. Like others who suffered loss during the storm, we experienced unprecedented levels of grace and love that we would not have otherwise known.

The spiritual strength gained from the trials of life often leads us to value the spiritual and emotional gems harvested from life's difficult places. When we survive periods of testing, we often grow to appreciate the value of hard times. As with Jesus, the angels of the Lord minister to us, and we exit our respective wilderness experiences in the wisdom and power of God.

Have you been battered by the trials of life? Make your best effort to find comfort in the Word of God, knowing that God will not put more on you than you can bear. Trust Him, especially when life baffles you. After all, God is indeed the Master of the Universe. His earlier creative words spoken at the beginning of time continue to call worlds into existence. Not to worry if the world you created has just been destroyed. By God's grace and power, and newfound confidence and resilience, you can construct a bigger and better world to be enjoyed not only in your lifetime but for generations to come. Remember, this is only a test!

Meditation 15:
Flowing in the Gift

From that time Jesus began to preach and say, "Repent, for the kingdom of heaven is at hand" (Matthew 4:17).

J esus launched His ministry as soon as His wilderness experience ended. Like many young ministers, He started first by preaching the message of His mentor John, a message of repentance that was eventually enhanced by Jesus' own God-ordained purpose.

As a pastor's daughter and church musician, I have had the wonderful privilege of watching many Christians find and pursue their divine purposes. The woman who was afraid to give a personal testimony before the congregation has now accepted a call to evangelize. The girl whose knees knocked, hands shook, and voice trembled as she held the microphone now leads the congregation confidently in praise and worship. The retired licensed vocational nurse who raised five children as a single parent and survived breast cancer and congestive heart failure now uses her life experiences to encourage women of all ages

and persuasions. The Vietnam-era veteran who lost a leg to diabetes and is on dialysis continues to uplift the audience with his melodious voice Sunday after Sunday.

Areas of weaknesses became perfect places for God's strength and power to shine brilliantly in the lives of these precious members. Their respective periods of testing are enhanced by a resolute flowing and sharing of their gifts in the sanctuary and without. I love watching them flow in their gift areas with a clear sense of purpose, commitment, and maturity. They encourage me by their faithfulness to surrender my gifts to God's will and purpose.

Consulting the Lord's guidance is especially important when we are multitalented, given the many directions our various gift areas might make available to us. We must entreat the Lord consistently to find out what He would have us do and when. Otherwise, our gifts risk being exploited or abused by others and even ourselves. We also risk exhausting ourselves by doing good works but outside of God's perfect will or timing. We must entreat the Lord about our projects in order to get maximum mileage out of our contributions. When we know who and whose we are, we are much less likely to be sidetracked by the charges of Pharisees or to spiral into despair for a lack of planning or counting up the cost for the projects we assume.

Because Jesus knew who He was and what His purpose was, He stated His desires clearly and acted decisively and consistently from the time He was confirmed. He flowed in His gift areas, performing everything prophesied earlier by the Prophet Isaiah, but He was balanced.

The same man who walked on water withdrew from His disciples to take a rest without having His divine ego bruised because He needed sleep. Flowing in one's gift areas requires time for rejuvenation, which for the Christian is best achieved through prayer, meditation, and time away from the hustle and bustle of everyday life. It means pulling away from our favorite television programs or activities to sit quietly at the feet of God in order to hear the still, small voice that offers guidance, reassurance, and often surprising revelations.

When we are truly flowing in our gift areas, we can wake up even out of deep slumber and calm the storm in someone else's life with a word spoken in season. I cannot count the times I have been encouraged by the words of a seasoned Christian who was simply sharing effortlessly out of his or her gift area. Or by someone who despite their compromised state of health was able to share words of grace and healing with me. I have experienced profound peace and intangible blessings from the residual contributions of loved ones who have gone on to be with the Lord.

This is especially true of my mother, the late First Lady Barbara Lessie Linton Kossie, whose commitment to the Lord continues to encourage me to seek and follow God's plan for my life. Her physical death notwithstanding, her contributions to my life are as real and rich as they have ever been, thanks to her embracing and using her spiritual gifts of love, kindness, and generosity to raise a strong family and nurture a thriving congregation. Her works continue to praise her in the gates as her biological and spiritual offspring flow in the gifts that God has planted inside them.

Are you flowing in your gift areas? If not, pray that God will help you remove any obstacles that threatened to dam the cool, fresh waters destined to emanate from your giftedness. Be sure to spend time in the presence and Word of God to ensure endless access to an immeasurable reservoir of peace, love, strength, and goodwill. Staying connected to His Majesty means flowing freely, not only in this world but in the world to come.

Meditation 16:
Transforming the Gift

Now after six days Jesus took Peter, James, and John his brother, led them up on a high mountain by themselves; and He was transfigured before them. His face shone like the sun, and his clothes became white as the light (Matthew 17: 1-2).

One of my favorite television shows in recent years was "Extreme Makeovers," where guests with longstanding physical imperfections were invited to undergo medical transformations. I sometimes shed tears of joy along with the women and men as they underwent their manmade miracles. The pain of the plastic surgeries and exercise programs they endured were accepted as a necessary part of the process of changing from undesirable to the desirable. Even as I celebrated their newfound beauty and watched their families and friends beam with joy, I always found myself thinking about the more important internal transformation we experience when we come to Christ.

The scripture admonishes, "And do not be conformed to this world but transformed by the renewing of your mind, that you may prove what is that good and acceptable and perfect will of God" (Romans 12:2). True transformation is based on our thought life: "As [a man] thinks in his heart, so is he" (Proverbs 23:7). The only way to experience the kind of internal transformation that God requires is to submit our thought life to God, as well as use the wonderful prescription for godly thinking that Paul outlined in scripture: "Finally, brethren, whatever things are noble, whatever things are just, whatever things are pure, whatever things are lovely, whatever things are of good report, if there is any virtue and if there is anything praiseworthy—meditate on these things" (Philippians 4:9).

I used these scriptures to align my thoughts with the will of God when I was going through a very difficult phase in my personal life. There was such a war going on in my mind that I decided to write out a literal checklist to determine whether I was going to think about a certain matter. I decided that whatever the thought, it needed to fulfill all the requirements outlined in the scripture. The longer I made a deliberate effort to filter my thoughts through the Word of God, the better I felt and the stronger I became.

Renewing the mind is not always easy, but it is always necessary, especially if we want to live vibrant, progressive Christian lives. Even Jesus Himself had to submit His thoughts to His Father. "Nevertheless not My will but Yours be done" (Luke 22:42) was His prayer. His purpose for coming to the earth depended on His decision to align His thoughts with the will of God. He died that we might live eternally with Him.

How is your thought life? Does your mind need to be renewed? Just humble yourself before the Lord, submit your "control center" to Him, and He will lead you to His perfect will for your life. The divine connection will be so dazzling that others will celebrate in awesome wonder the things God is doing in and through you. Let the transformation begin!

Meditation 17:
Surrendering the Gift

O My Father, if it is possible, let this cup pass from Me; nevertheless, not as I will, but as You will (Matthew 26: 39).

In a culture where winning and determination are highly prized and often measured in dollar signs, the word "surrender" sounds counterproductive. To many it connotes quitting—the last thing go-getters are willing to do. Christians are nonetheless required by the tenets of their faith to surrender all to the will and purpose of God. Surrendering is often not an event but rather a process that is constantly engaged over the course of the Christian journey. It requires embracing gift areas wholeheartedly, planting talents with gratitude, and doing so for the glory and honor of God, not for our own glory or that of others, but for the Lord.

We must surrender our gifts to God daily because while they are God-given and irrevocable, they can be grossly misapplied or misused in the absence of spiritual deference to God's will. This fact is clearly evident in the case of Paul the Apostle, who prior to his transformation on the road to Damascus had terrified many a Christian by misusing his gifts to the utter destruction of many.

As Jesus demonstrated in His act of submission to His Father's will, surrendering to ultimate wisdom puts us in the ultimate position to do the greatest possible good through our gifts and talents. As God is omniscient, omnipresent, and omnipotent, He is most capable of knowing when, where, and how our gifts will be most "effective," a term that God may define very differently from us.

From time to time, the Lord allows us to feel the weight of His will and purpose on our lives or the burden of the assignment we have been called to complete. When we perceive the magnitude of what He has called us to do, or when our Peter-like faith to walk on water is suddenly challenged by an unexpected wave of menacing events, we begin to sink under pressure and cry out for deliverance. We begin to think, "Lord, maybe I am not cut out for this after all. Who was I to believe you for the impossible?" But once we remember to wave a white flag of surrender to God's purpose, we begin once again to find peace that passes all understanding despite the circumstances facing us.

This is what happened with Jesus as He prepared to give the greatest gift of all—His life—so that you and I might live. So in tune had He become with His Father's will by the end of His assignment that He was able to focus on the spiritual needs of His enemies despite their being the source of His pain. He prayed, "Father, forgive them, for they know not what they do" (Luke 23:34).

Our ability to surrender to God's will, even when doing so means enduring great personal discomfort and duress, is among the highest spiritual heights we can achieve. Those who truly surrender to God testify that giving their all to Him for His glory led them to fields greener and richer than anything they could have achieved without surrendering their gifts and talents to God's divine purpose.

Have you surrendered your gifts to God? Is He being glorified by the talents He has placed in your life? Have you asked Him lately whether He is pleased by the gifts you are offering to Him? Surrendering is hardly easy, but it is absolutely necessary if we want our works to really count. In our relationship with God, "giving in" to His will is always good because God is ultimate wisdom and authority. Winning is the only possibility when we surrender our will to His, even when it may not seem so to us or others. As the enduring prayerful chant of the Church of God in Christ admonishes, just tell Him "Yes!" and everything will work out well for all concerned.

Meditation 18:
Resurrecting the Gift

But the angel answered and said to the women, "Do not be afraid, for I know that you seek Jesus who was crucified. He is not here; for He is risen, as He said" (Matthew 28: 5).

Women who loved Jesus were the first to receive the message that He had fulfilled the prophetic announcement of His resurrection, a moment that he Himself had foretold. They had come to anoint with spices the body of their Blessed Friend whose death they had accepted. They came looking for the Jesus who had surrendered His will to the will of His Father and had been crucified. But they learned from a divine messenger that Jesus was alive. What appeared at first to have been a robbery turned out to be a resurrection. Perhaps, like Jesus, you have surrendered your will to the Lord and seem to have come to a dead end. Perhaps others who know and love you also believe your dream will never be realized and now anoint your faded hope with fragrant oils and spices. Just keep standing on the word of God and believing for a fresh, miraculous start. All things are possible to those who believe (Mark 9:23).

I lived through the birth, death, and resurrection of my music ministry. I began playing for my father's church when I was about thirteen years old, and continue to do so despite intermittent educational and professional journeys to various places. I loved music and often played and prayed throughout the night.

In the wee hours of the morning, the Lord would give me solos, choral renditions, anthems, and praise and worship tunes that I would share with various soloists and singing groups at church. I started out playing the piano and graduated to the organ, where I directed the choir and sometimes led songs or sang solos.

Because the Lord had spoken to me through various prophets that I was going to record, I was more than happy to keep attending church and composing music because I knew what lay ahead. When matters did not materialize like I thought, I gradually grew despondent and lost my joy as one door after the other that I attempted to enter slammed shut in my face.

So off track, so I thought, I had become that I found myself teaching history, a subject that I had vowed as a child never to teach. My real heart's desire was to dedicate myself to music full time. I cried myself to sleep many nights about not having listened to my mother, who had encouraged me to earn a music degree during my undergraduate years. I was so confident in my gift at that time that I did not think I needed one to achieve my dream, particularly given that very few gospel greats had gone through academic channels to achieve their dreams.

I was so sure that God was going to move quickly that I bypassed my first opportunity to obtain a degree in music, although I took as many courses as I could. Years later I realized what appeared to have been a mistake and started trying to obtain a Bachelor's degree in music from TSU where years later I served as an adjunct professor of French and eventually a tenured professor of history, my current position.

I was doing well at TSU and enjoying my experience, but the bottom fell out financially and quite unexpectedly. I was informed that the academic scholarship I had received for the fall would not be renewed in the spring because I had already obtained a Master's degree, although in another field. The well-paying part-time job I held with Continuing Studies at Rice University was suspended to avoid my exceeding the 20-hour-per-week work limit established for part-time employees. This double blow forced me to return to the secondary classroom to teach, a full-time job that I knew was incompatible with my new aim.

I was disappointed, but I accepted that the sudden turn of events could not have occurred without God's approval. Determined to move forward with my pursuit of music, I earned money and began saving to record in the studio. I felt that I had to give the Lord something to work with, so I started to pay for studio time. When I was in the middle of the project, Apostle Daniel Allen of New Jersey and a longtime friend of the family gave me a prophetic word that I know could only have come from God because he knew nothing of my ventures.

He was leaving the sanctuary and returned to say with his crisp Jersey accent, "Sis. Karen. I don't know what the Lord means by what He is saying, but you will understand. He says when it's time you won't have to pay for it." My mouth fell open. I knew exactly what the prophet was talking about because I was putting all of my free time and energy into the project.

I surrendered to the will of God but became gradually saddened when the opportunity to record never came. I recall the very painful moment I declared, without consulting the Chief Physician, that my dream was dead. Shrouded in doubt and without clear direction, I could not see then how the Lord could get anything out of my chronic inertia. So, I declared the dream over, finished, done with. I mourned for days, months, even years because my beloved dream deferred had dried up like a raisin in the sun. I even found it difficult to listen to gospel music because doing so reacquainted me with the pain of my unfulfilled dreams. I played for services out of duty, but my heart was not there like it had been.

As the years rolled on, I understood why the recording opportunity had not come. Simply put, I was not ready. Singing for me was more talent than gift; I needed to work at. Most importantly, I needed to learn the basics of breathing, and how to take care of my vocal instrument. Thanks to my short encounter at TSU, I had learned to my surprise that I was a soprano—a definite challenge for a woman aspiring to sing gospel music. I also learned about decorum and a host of other issues important to vocalist and musicians.

I met a professional musician and producer who listened to my demo tapes and pointed out the flaws in the production. He also cautioned me about the stylistic ambiguity in my voice. Admittedly, my soprano voice was suspended between opera and jazz. I therefore needed more vocal training to bridge the gap. I eventually knew I had to have been making progress when the now late Rosalyn Brunswick McDuffy heard me sing at a banquet and encouraged me to record.

In due course, I realized I had been my own problem. I had inadvertently interpreted the term "music ministry" and its historical trajectory according to my own wishes, not the Lord's. For example, the late Prophetess Eddie B. Leadon, pastor and founder of Miracle House, Freeport, TX, told me that she saw me singing in England. I was elated. I imagined the crowds, lights, and applause.

Within a year or so of the prophecy, I actually did sing in England, but to a very subdued group of about fifteen people in a small fellowship hall on an icy Sunday morning. To top matters off, not a single person of the fifteen clapped when I finished my rendition; applauding solo performances in church was apparently not part of their liturgical tradition.

Other ministers had told me that they saw me singing before thousands. I was delighted with every pronouncement and imagined myself in concert with CDs, flyers, and postcards bedecking a table celebrating my new releases. True to prophecy, I sang before thousands but usually with special-event or holiday concert choirs. In fact, the only time I went anything close to solo was at a Nicole C. Mullins Christmas concert held in The Woodlands, TX, and sponsored by Houston's 89.3 KSBJ radio station.

As time and chance would have it, concert organizers needed a volunteer to lead the audience in "Joy to the World" before the event began. My younger sister and KSBJ personality Kim Kossie knew I was in attendance and declared me the "ram in the bush." What a willing and happy ram I was.

By this time, thanks to much prayer and healing I had begun to laugh at the degree to which I had embellished various prophetic affirmations with my own desires, when God clearly had something else in mind. His thoughts were definitely not mine. By God's grace, I had begun to say, "Lord, if I never release a CD, I thank you for the music ministry I have at my church, where I am destined to glorify Your name in music and song."

My faith had grown stronger, because a few years earlier I had fleeced the Lord about my musical gift, and He had provided me with an experience that is still wonderful to recall. My question to Him was, "Lord, how are You going to fulfill Your promises to me about music now that I am working on a PhD in history?"

It was 1996. I was more than delighted to head to Paris, France, for an interdisciplinary conference titled "African American Music in Paris" and held at La Sorbonne. The conference was sponsored by Harvard University's DuBois Institute and the Collegium on African American Research (CAAR), an association of European scholars interested in African American history and culture. With celebrated scholars and musicians slated to attend, including Henry Louis "Skip" Gates and Quincy Jones, the conference promised to feed the intellect and tickle the ear.

Just before I left, my father told me as he prayed for me that I was going to have a very blessed trip— that God was going to do something very special for me. I was a doctoral candidate at the time. Other than meet the man of my dreams, I could not imagine what that would be, but I accepted the prophecy by faith.

At the conference I met a Jamaican designer who after our encounter went to the beauty salon, where she told everyone about an African-American woman she had met from Houston who spoke fluent French. In the same shop at the same time, Sharon Peterson, a childhood friend and former fellow music student, recognized me by the woman's description and asked the woman to put us in touch with each other. Unbelievable!

Sharon and I chose to meet at the Sunday Jazz/Gospel brunch held at a café off the Champs-Elysées. As we listened to the music, one of the African-American jazz vocalists whom I had told I could play asked me to accompany her as she sang Thomas Dorsey's classic "Take My Hand Precious Lord" and other gospel favorites. In an unexpected moment and an unlikely place—a café in Paris, I felt divine energy enter the top of my head and flow in an instant to my shoulders, down my arms, to my fingertips, through the keyboard, and toward the audience. In perfect synchronicity, the audience stood to its feet and began clapping. After the renditions were over, audience members started approaching and asking where I had learned to play and if I had considered playing professionally. The owner of the club gave me an open invitation to play at the club whenever I liked.

The Spirit of the Lord whispered in my ear, "That's how it can happen!" In a moment, in the twinkling of an eye, God demonstrated that He could transform a musician from a church in Houston's Fifth Ward into an internationally acclaimed virtuoso, for a minute or millennium. It is His choice.

If that were not encouraging enough, Sharon, unbeknown to me, had approached everyone who had come to congratulate me and invited them on the spot to a surprise party in my honor, which was held in her posh apartment in the Cinquième Arrondissement, thanks to the great international job she held with one of the most popular companies on the planet. I was floored.

She and I shopped about for my party and caught up on each other's adventuresome lives. Within a couple of hours, she had transformed her apartment into a banquet hall adorned with a colorful array of flowers, fresh delicacies, fruits, and viands from a nearby épicerie. Sharon's elegant surroundings, grace, and charm made me and the twenty odd guests invited feel more than special. We all laughed and chatted for hours about music and life in the City of Light. My spirits were so high by the end of the evening that I could have flown back to Houston without boarding the plane.

I was so humbled that the Lord had chosen Sharon, a dear childhood friend, to create this very special moment in a very special place. She was clearly an instrument of His service then and certainly now as a minister's wife. I knew God was reiterating through my friend just how quickly He can change our circumstances. At the same time, I understood intrinsically that the fullness of time had still not come. He was still working His plan—one that renewed my faith in new beginnings from that miraculous moment on.

Not to worry then if the cherished gift you surrendered to God appears to be dying right before your eyes and even the eyes of others. Never mind how long your dream has lain dormant. Keep believing God for resurrection. For the power of God is infinitely capable of bringing life in an instant and sustaining life in the direst of circumstances. Remember that all things are possible if we just believe (Mark 9:23).

Meditation 19:

Glorifying the Gift

All authority has been given to Me in heaven and on earth. Go therefore and make disciples of all the nations, baptizing them in the name of the Father and the Son and the Holy Spirit, teaching them to observe all things that I have commanded you; and lo, I am with you always, even to the end of the age (Matthew 28:18).

As the above scripture affirms, the ultimate purpose for our various gifts is to glorify God in this world and the world to come. Through his birth, ministry, death, and resurrection, Jesus has provided us with a perfect model for glorifying God with our gifts. To glorify God implies worshipping and praising Him with our various gifts, callings, and talents. It means believing wholeheartedly that "we have this treasure in earthen vessels, that the excellency of the power may be of God, and not of us" (2 Corinthians 4:7). It means being thoroughly committed to sharing God's love with others throughout the world for His glory and honor.

Many modern Christians have taken Christ's words to heart. They are engaged in the five-fold ministries and contemporary representations of the same. Some have taken the Christian message to Hollywood, while others have found creative ways to use the Internet to share the love of God. The harvest is so ripe that the kingdom of God is in constant need of laborers with various gifts and talents to lead others to Christ through the love of God.

Glorifying God with our gifts requires stirring them up (2 Timothy 1:6), or keeping them active, invigorated, and in ready use. Worshipping Him with our talents requires saying "no" to fear and "yes" to God's boundless power and love, as well as to the inner strength and resolve that come with both. Stirring up our gifts also requires the support of our spiritual leaders, whose prayers help to activate and sustain God's gifts in us.

I praise God for the support I continue to receive from Bishop Kossie, my father and pastor, as well as from the many ministers and laypersons God has used over the course of my life to keep me stirred in my various gift areas and talents to write, play, sing, compose, or teach. Whenever I feel ineffective or outspent, God always sends an unexpected someone to kindle the waning flames in my life. I am always careful to let them know how much I value their kind words and prayers.

Are you praising and worshipping God through the gifts He has graciously given you? Have you asked your spiritual leader to bless your godly endeavors? Have you thanked him or her personally for their prayers and encouraging support?

Joseph, Mary, and Jesus together provided us

with an excellent model for bearing and sharing our gifts for God's glory and honor. May God anoint us to glean fully and freely from the Holy Family's example of faith and obedience—one that generated a Revival so powerful that it continues to bring healing, restoration, and infinite hope.

Are you ready to bear and share the gifts God has placed inside you? Are you ready to glorify Him and declare His Majesty through the work He has chosen you to do? If so, let us pray together:

Father God,

I thank You for the precious gifts You have given me to glorify Your name. I surrender these expressions of unmerited grace and favor to Your divine will and purpose.

May I always be guided by the light of your love and never by fear or doubt. Help me to lay aside anything that will hinder my accomplishing Your perfect will.

May I always remember to entreat You throughout my journey so that I accomplish the greatest good for Your glory, honor, and praise—not mine.

Thank You for the grace and humility to bear and share Your many gifts with whomever and wherever You deem necessary.

Dear Lord, be magnified in all that I say and do. Be glorified in my gifts every minute of every day, now and forevermore. In Jesus' name I pray. Amen.

Appendix I

Howard Gardner's Theory of Multiple Intelligences

Intelligence	Core Operations
Linguistic	Syntax, phonology, semantics, pragmatics
Musical	Pitch, rhythm, timbre
Logical-mathematical	Number categorization, relations
Spatial	Accurate mental visualization, mental transformation of images
Bodily-kinesthetic	Control of one's body, control in handling objects
Interpersonal	Awareness of others' feelings, emotions, goals, motivations
Intrapersonal	Awareness of one's own feelings, emotions, goals motivations
Naturalist	Recognition and classification of objects in the environment

Cited at http://pzharvard.edu/sumit/MISUMIT.HTM, Last accessed, January 2004.

Appendix II

Exilic Experiences of the Holy Family and African Americans Compared

TRANSPLANTED	
Holy Family: "Whole"	**Enslaved Africans: "Separated"**
✓ From danger to safety	✓ From safety to danger (captured in times of peace) ✓ From danger to even greater danger (captured in times of war
✓ Social Status: Free	✓ Free and Enslaved (Early Explorers) ✓ Enslaved (Slave Trade)
✓ Exile lasted approximately 3 ½ years	✓ Enslaved approximately 3 ½ centuries; legally oppressed for at least 66 years (Jim Crow)
✓ Family relocated as a unit	✓ Families dislocated and scattered
✓ Native language preserved and new language acquired	✓ Native languages lost and new ones acquired (Portuguese, Spanish, English, French, Dutch)
✓ Family well-received and protected	✓ Families exploited, but many survived and thrived despite the hardship

✓ Birthed the Coptic Church of Egypt, which takes pride in establishing the "first Christian church in the world"	✓ Birthed the "Black Church," including the African Methodist Episcopal Church, National Baptist Convention, Church of God in Christ, Church of God Pillar and Ground of the Truth, etc.
✓ Gifts survived and new ones acquired	✓ Gifts survived and new ones acquired

Appendix III

Flight into Egypt and Returning From Egypt

Many western artists painted works depicting the Holy Family's flight into Egypt. But I found only one painting highlighting the Holy Family's return from Egypt: Jacob Jordaens' "The Return of the Holy Family from Egypt." I found no western European works of art to date that highlighted the Holy Family's sojourn in Egypt. This absence of western paintings can easily be explained: The painters were not there, but the Egyptians were. The Holy Family's exilic experience unfolded outside the historical and geographical scope of western Europeans. Divisions between the Catholic Church and the Orthodox Church may have also created the subsequent silencing of the Egyptian Christian testimony in the western world. Consider the following western artists and the titles of their paintings:

Artist	Title of Painting
Albrecht Altdorfer	The Rest on the Flight to Egypt
Melchior Broederlam	Presentation in the Temple and Flight into Egypt
Jan Brueghel the Elder	Forest's Edge (Flight to Egypt)
Caravaggio	The Rest on the Flight to Egypt
Correggio	The Rest on the Flight to Egypt
Lucas Cranach the Elder	Rest on the Flight to Egypt
Gerard David	A Rest During the Flight into Egypt
Duccio di Buoninsegna	Maesta: The Flight into Egypt
Anthony van Dyck	The Rest on the Flight to Egypt
Giotto	Flight into Egypt
Jacob Jordaens	The Return of the Holy Family from Egypt
Bartolome Esteban Murillo	Rest on the Flight to Egypt
Nicolas Poussin	Rest on the Flight to Egypt
Rembrandt	St. Joseph's Dream
Jean-Antoine Watteau	Rest on the Flight into Egypt

See http://www.abcgallery.com/religion/flight.html

Appendix IV

The Beginning of Life: Pregnancy through Preschool

By the time the Holy Family departed from Egypt, Jesus had achieved the following skills:

Age	Motor	Social	Verbal and cognitive
3 years	▪ Rides a tricycle ▪ Undresses and partially dresses without help ▪ Identifies some colors ▪ Climbs stairs using alternate feet ▪ Stacks 9 blocks ▪ Cuts paper with scissors ▪ Copies a circle 0	▪ Has a sense of self as male or female (gender identity) ▪ Usually achieves bowel and bladder control ▪ Can spend part of the day with adults other than parents (e.g., in preschool setting)	▪ Uses about 900 words in speech ▪ Understands about 3,500 words ▪ Speaks in complete sentences (e.g., I can do it myself)
4 years	▪ Catches a ball with arms ▪ Dresses independently, using buttons and zippers (e.g., brushes teeth) ▪ Hops on one foot ▪ Copies a cross +	▪ Begins to play cooperatively with other children ▪ Engages in role playing (e.g., I'll be the daddy, you be the mommy) ▪ May have imaginary companions ▪ Has curiosity about sex differences (e.g., plays "doctor" with other children ▪ Has nightmares and transient phobias (e.g., of "monsters")	▪ Shows good verbal self-expression (e.g., can tell detailed stories) ▪ Comprehends and uses prepositions (e.g., under, above)

Cited in Barbara Fadem, *Behavioral Science*, 3rd Edition, Lippincott Williams and Wilkins: *The Science Review*, 2000, p. 7.

100

---

[1] See Appendix I.
[2] See Appendix II. The Holy Family's sojourn in Egypt provides an excellent opportunity to compare the Holy Family's experience and that of enslaved Africans in the Americas.
[3] See Appendix III. The chart contains a list of European artists who depicted the Flight to Egypt.
[4] See Appendix IV. The chart details the growth stages Jesus had achieved by the time his family returned to Israel.

Printed in the United States
137778LV00003B/32/P